Geographical Readers for Elementary Schools

THE LONDON GEOGRAPHICAL SERIES.

GEOGRAPHICAL READERS

FOR

ELEMENTARY SCHOOLS.

BY

CHARLOTTE M. MASON,

AUTHORESS OF " THE FORTY SHIRES, THEIR HISTORY, SCENERY, ARTS,
AND LEGENDS."

BOOK I. FOR STANDARD II.

ELEMENTARY GEOGRAPHY.

With Illustrations and Maps.

LONDON:

EDWARD STANFORD, 55, CHARING CROSS, S.W.

1881.

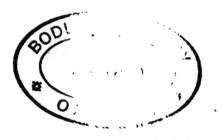

To "Otters."

The writer begs affectionately to inscribe these Books to Teachers trained at the Otter Memorial College, in memory of very pleasant hours spent with intelligent and responsive Classes.

PREFACE.

THIS little book is written on the lines laid down by the Old Code for the Geography of Standard II. It is confined to very simple reading lessons upon "the Form and Motions of the Earth, the Points of the Compass, the Meaning of a Map: Definitions." The writer is unable to conceive of any other course of early lessons so practically useful and necessary.

The shape and motions of the earth are fundamental ideas — however difficult to grasp.

Geography should be learned chiefly from maps, and the child should begin the study by learning "the meaning of a map," and how to use it.

These subjects are well fitted to form an

attractive introduction to the study of Geography: some of them should awaken the delightful interest which attaches in a child's mind to that which is wonderful—incomprehensible. The Map lessons should lead to mechanical efforts, equally delightful. It is only when presented to the child for the first time in the form of stale knowledge and foregone conclusions that the facts taught in these lessons appear dry and repulsive to him.

An effort is made in the following pages to treat the subject with the sort of sympathetic interest and freshness which attracts children to a new study.

A short summary of the chief points in each reading lesson is given in the form of questions and answers.

Easy verses, illustrative of the various subjects, are introduced, in order that the children may connect pleasant poetic fancies with the phenomena upon which "Geography" so much depends.

It is hoped that these reading lessons may

afford intelligent teaching, even in the hands of a young pupil teacher.

The first ideas of Geography—the lessons on "Place"—which should make the child observant of local geography, of the features of his own neighbourhood, its heights and hollows and level lands, its streams and ponds—should be conveyed vivâ voce. At this stage, a class-book cannot take the place of an intelligent teacher. Probably, however, this kind of matter is usually taught to the children in Standard I., or to the elder children of an Infant-school.

C. M. M.

CONTENTS.

———

GEOGRAPHICAL READERS.

BOOK I. FOR STANDARD II.

LESSON I.

HOW ALL THINGS PRAISE THE LORD.

SUN, moon, and stars, by day and night,
At God's commandment give us light;
And when we wake, and while we sleep,
Their watch, like guardian angels, keep.

The bright blue sky above our head,
The soft green earth on which we tread,
The ocean rolling round the land,
Were made by God's almighty hand.

Sweet flowers that hill and dale adorn,
Fair fruit trees, fields of grass and corn,
The clouds that rise, the showers that fall,
The winds that blow—God sent them all.

The beasts that graze with downward eye,
The birds that perch, and sing, and fly,
The fishes swimming in the sea,
God's creatures are as well as we.

B

But us He formed for better things,
As servants of the King of kings,
With lifted hands and open face,
And thankful heart to seek His grace.
MONTGOMERY.

LESSON II.

OUR WORLD.

PART I.

PERHAPS you have not yet thought much
about places far from the town or village
where your home is. No doubt you have
heard of the wonderful sights of London, if
you have not seen them, and you know that
London and many other towns are in our
own country, England. Perhaps, too, you
have friends who have travelled, and who
speak of far-away places they have seen.
And you may have thought, as you listened,
how very big the world must be to hold so
many places!

Our wonderful, beautiful world is very large
and very full; with more people and places

and things in it than you can ever know about. Indeed, there are many parts of it which nobody has seen yet, though brave men often make difficult and very dangerous journeys to find out and explore these unknown places. But, after all, the strange thing is, that our world must come to an end somewhere. Have you ever thought of that? It was a great puzzle to learned men who lived long ago, and who did not know so much about some things as you may learn before the end of this lesson. They knew the world was not everywhere; that the sun and moon which shine above us are not part of the world, but are a great way off. So they said, Why do we never come to the end of the world? If we journey on over land and sea for years, surely we should come to the end then? And what is the end like? Should we fall off the edge, just as a cup might fall off the edge of a table?

At last it was discovered that people never came to the end of the world on account of its shape. There are certain things we use which you might run your finger along all day without ever coming to an edge. Round things, such as balls or oranges have no edge, no end. And our world is round. It is more the shape of an orange than of a ball, because it is a little bit flat at what we may call the top and bottom.

This was a wonderful thing to find out. You can see that a ball is round; even if it were a ball as big as the house, you could see enough of it to know its shape. But only God above can see the whole of this huge world; how then could men discover its shape?

You would not understand all the reasons which prove that the world is round, but three are easy enough. The captain of a ship found out, that, by sailing on and on, and never turning back, he came at last to the very place he had started from. Try that plan on a straight table, and you will find that the farther you go, the farther you will be from your starting place. Try on a ball which you have first stuck a pin into for a mark. After you have moved your finger half way round the ball, the farther you go, the nearer you get to the pin, until at last you touch it, and have reached

again the point you started from. As people
now very often sail round the world in this
way, we know that the world is round in one
direction. The other two reasons we shall
find in the fourth lesson.

LESSON III.

THE SAILOR-BOY'S GOSSIP.

You say, dear mamma, it is good to be talking
  With those who will kindly endeavour to teach,
And I think I have learnt something while I was
    walking
  Along with the sailor-boy down on the beach.

He told me of lands where he soon will be going,
  Where humming-birds scarcely are bigger than
    bees,
Where the mace and the nutmeg together are
    growing,
  And cinnamon formeth the bark of some trees.

He told me that islands far out in the ocean
  Are mountains of coral that insects have made,
And I freely confess I had hardly a notion
  That insects could work in the way that he said.

He spoke of wide deserts where the sand-clouds are
    flying,
    No shade for the brow, and no grass for the feet;
Where camels and travellers often lie dying,
    Gasping for water and scorching with heat.

CORAL ISLAND IN THE PACIFIC.

He told me of places away in the East,
    Where topaz, and ruby, and sapphires are found;
Where you never are safe from the snake and the
    beast,
    For the serpent and tiger and jackal abound.

I thought our own Thames was a very great stream,
    With its waters so fresh and its currents so strong ;
But how tiny our largest of rivers must seem
    To those he had sailed on, three thousand miles long.

He speaks, dear mamma, of so many strange places,
 With people who neither have cities nor kings,
Who wear skins on their shoulders, paint on their
  faces,
 And live on the spoils which their hunting-field
  brings.

Oh! I long, dear mamma, to learn more of these
  stories,
 From books that are written to please and to teach,
And I wish I could see half the curious glories
 The sailor-boy told me of down on the beach.

ELIZA COOK.

LESSON IV.

OUR WORLD.

PART II.

WE cannot go round the world for ourselves,
but there are some ways of knowing its shape
which we can try.

If you are on a hill or tower, so high that you can see over all the buildings near, and beyond them as far as the eye can reach, you will find that you are in the middle of a great circle or ring. Everywhere, all round you, the world and the sky seem to touch one another. It is not that they really do so; but the eye can see no farther, because the world, everywhere beyond this circle, dips down out of sight, as the sides of an orange might to a fly on the top. The place where the earth and sky seem to meet is called the *horizon*.

All over the world, wherever anybody stands so that he can have an unbroken view, he finds himself standing in the middle of such a circle.

That the surface of the world is everywhere rounded in this way is one proof that the world is round; or rather, that it is a *sphere*, a name given to objects which are round in every direction like a ball. *Globe* is another name given to objects of this shape.

As the world is rounded everywhere, this roundness hides very distant objects from view, as a hill might. Thus you may sometimes see the top of an object when its lower part is hidden by the round swell. The dome of Saint Paul's may be seen from a great distance; while the doors would be hidden by this rounding of the earth, even if there were no buildings between you and them.

The best way to understand this is to stand on the sea-shore and watch a ship just coming into sight from below the horizon. The sea looks so flat, it is hard to believe there is any roundness there, and yet, something rises between you and the ship. Instead of seeing the whole of her, you see only the slight masts. The large heavy hull, the part which you would expect to show most clearly in the distance, is quite hidden from view.

What hides it? The rounding of the waters. The sea, which covers part of the world's surface, has everywhere just the same curve or roundness as the land.

Questions on Lessons II. and IV.

1. What is the shape of the world?—Round, like an orange; that is, a little flattened at the top and bottom.

2. Give one reason for supposing that the world is round?—A ship may arrive at the place she started from by sailing right on without ever turning back.

3. Does this prove that the world is round in every direction like a ball?—No; only that it is round in the direction in which the ship sails.

4. Why do we say the world is a sphere or globe? —Because it is round in every direction, like a ball.

5. How is this proved?—When nothing hides the view to a great distance, the land sinks out of sight all round us, and we are standing in the middle of a circle.

6. What causes this effect?—The rounding of the surface of the world ; we cannot see straight on as if it were flat.

7. Does this prove that the world is a sphere?— Yes; because the same effect may be seen in every part of the world ; it is round in every direction.

8. What is this circle called?—The horizon ; the world and sky seem to meet all round.

9. Can the roundness of the world be seen in any other way?—Yes; it rises between us and objects at a distance, hiding the lower parts of them from view.

10. Mention such an object?—A ship coming in to land : when she first appears we cannot see her hull.

LESSON V.

THE STAR.

Twinkle, twinkle little star ;
How I wonder what you are!
Up above the world so high,
Like a diamond in the sky.

When the blazing sun is gone,
When he nothing shines upon,
Then you show your little light—
Twinkle, twinkle, all the night.

Then the traveller in the dark,
Thanks you for your tiny spark ;
He could not see which way to go
If you did not twinkle so.

In the dark blue sky you keep,
Yet often through my window peep ;
For you never shut your eye
Till the sun is in the sky.

As your bright but tiny spark
Lights the traveller in the dark,
Though I know not what you are,
Twinkle, twinkle little star.

JANE TAYLOR,

LESSON VI.

OUR WORLD AND OTHER WORLDS.

PART I.

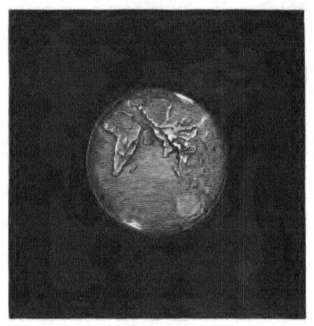

THE EARTH.

ABOUT three hundred years ago, there lived a wise man, named Galileo, who spent his nights in watching the stars, and in considering how they moved. Perhaps you think the stars are little shining lamps, lit up in the sky every night, which do not move at all. Galileo knew better; and, in his long night-watches, he found out some wonderful things about our world which you shall hear.

Not that he was exactly the first to make these discoveries. But Galileo was among the first who wished to make others as wise as himself. He wrote his wonderful secrets in a book and taught the people. Alas, his books were burned, and he, himself, was imprisoned. Men said his strange tales were not true, and were angry with the man who wished to teach them.

Have you noticed that things look smaller and smaller the farther you are from them? That a kite flies up, till it looks like a speck; that a man in the distance looks no bigger than a child? Get far enough off, and the very largest thing looks no bigger than a dot. Even our own great world would seem no larger than one of the stars in the sky if we could get far enough off to see it so small; which we never can, because we cannot get out of our own world.

Galileo's wonderful discovery was, that nearly all the stars we see in the sky are as

large, some of them many times as large, as
our world.   They are so far off that they
look small to us, just as our world would look
if seen from a star.

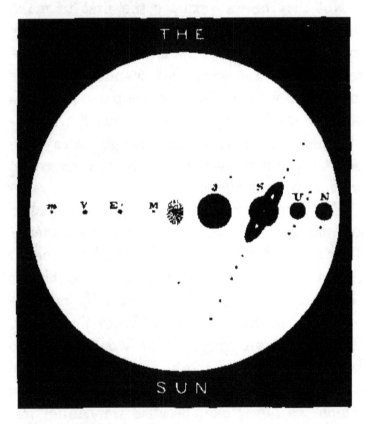

Then he went on to tell that our world is
really a kind of star, which, with seven others
something like it, is always going round the

sun.   These eight stars, which are always
wandering round the sun, are called planets,
a word which means wanderers.   Our world
is a planet, and its name is Earth; another
planet is called Venus; and each of the other
planets has a name of its own which you may
learn some day.

But, you say, the stars all shine like lamps;
how then can our earth look like a star?   It
is not on fire.   It is true that most of the
stars do shine and burn like the sun, but
these eight planets, of which our earth is one,
shine in another way.

Have you ever seen the windows of a house
look red and bright when the sun was shining
on them in the evening?   Sometimes you
would think the house was on fire, they look
in such a blaze; but it is only the light of
the sun which they are sending back, or
reflecting.   On a sun-shiny, hot day by the
sea-side you can hardly bear to look at anything.   Water and houses and pavement
dazzle you so with the sun's light, which
they are reflecting, that it is almost as bad as
trying to look at the sun himself.

If we were off our earth, far, far away, up

in space, we should not see houses, trees, and
water, but just a ball shining all over with
the light of the sun, which it is giving back
or reflecting. And that is how it is that
these eight planets, and our moon also, shine
like bright stars, though they are not really
bright themselves. They send back, or re-
flect, the bright light of the sun.

LESSON VII.

OUR WORLD AND OTHER WORLDS.

PART II.

THE great sun is very glorious and beautiful,
and is always pouring out floods of light and
of fierce heat. His light gives day to all
the planets; and his heat enables corn to
grow upon our earth, and men to live there;
and makes warm summer days when children
may play in the fields.

But his fiercest heat does not come to our
earth; we are far, far away from the great
fire of the sun; and only get the gentle

warmth which makes our world pleasant.
Some parts of the world get much more of
the sun's heat than others; why they do so,
you will know soon; but it is nowhere
scorching hot. Everywhere, nearly, people
and animals may live, and plants grow; and
the sun is a kind friend which gives life and
pleasure to all living things.

Day and night, never resting for a moment,
the eight planets are continually moving round
the sun. When the journey is finished they
begin again, silent, punctual, never tired;
so punctual are they, that astronomers (the
wise men like Galileo who study the stars)
know just in what part of the sky to look for
a planet at any time. And it comes—more
true to time than a railway train, but without
any blowing of whistles or ringing of bells,
without any bustle or noise or smoke. And
the astronomers are filled with delight to see
how well these wonderful works of God obey
the law He has given them.

The eight planets do not travel round the
sun side by side. Some are much farther
from the sun than our earth. Some are
nearer to him. As each one keeps at a

regular distance from the sun all through
its journey, the more distant the planet is,
the longer is the time it takes to finish its
course.   The length of our year is 365 days,

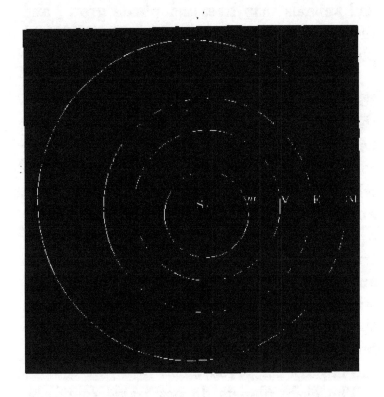

but the planet Saturn, which is much farther
from the sun than the earth is, has a year
nearly thirty times as long as ours. That is
to say, he has a far larger circle to move

round, so it takes him nearly thirty times as long as it takes the earth to go round the sun. Supposing each of the planets left a shining track which we could see as it went on its course, there would be eight shining circles round the sun at different distances from him. These would show us the *orbits* or paths of the planets. The path our earth takes through space in her journey round the sun is her orbit. Not that there is any real path or waymark of any kind for her to follow. Yet, year after year, she journeys over the same course, and never gets nearer to the sun or farther from him. Should she lose her way by any chance, and get nearer to the sun, terrible things would follow. Trees, grass, and houses would all blaze up; the very hills and ground would burn; and our whole world would become a great fire, kindled by the fierce heat of the sun. But there is no chance in the matter. God keeps the earth and the other planets moving round in their own places by two wonderful laws which cannot be broken. But you are too young to understand about these yet.

Questions on Lessons VI. and VII.

1. What discovery did Galileo make?—That our world is a planet.

2. What is a planet?—A body that looks bright like a star, and travels round the sun.

3. How do planets shine?—By reflecting the sun's light. They have none in themselves.

4. Is not our world larger than the stars and planets?—A great deal smaller than the stars, which are very far away: smaller than most of the planets.

5. What is our world's name as a planet?—Earth.

6. How long is our year?—Rather more than 365 days.

7. Is there any reason why our year should be 365 days in length?—That is the time the earth takes to perform her journey round the sun.

8. What is the path she takes round the sun called?—Her orbit.

LESSON VIII.

THE SUNSHINE.

I LOVE the sunshine everywhere,
  In wood, and field, and glen;
I love it in the busy haunts
  Of town-imprisoned men.

I love it when it streameth in
   The humble cottage door,
And casts the chequered casement-shade
   Upon the red brick floor.

I love it where the children lie
   Deep in the clovery grass,
To watch among the twining roots
   The gold-green beetles pass.

How beautiful, where dragon-flies
   Are wondrous to behold,
With rainbow wings of gauzy pearl,
   And bodies blue and gold!

How beautiful on harvest-slopes,
   To see the sunshine lie;
Or on the paler reapèd fields,
   Where yellow shocks stand high!

Oh! yes; I love the sunshine!
   Like kindness or like mirth,
Upon a human countenance,
   Is sunshine on the earth!

Upon the earth; upon the sea;
   And through the crystal air,
On piled up clouds; the gracious sun
   Is glorious everywhere.
             MARY HOWITT.

LESSON IX.

DAY AND NIGHT.

THE earth not only travels round the sun in a year, but the whole of that time it is itself turning round, or rotating. Just so, a top, while spinning quickly, might at the same time move along the floor. Turn round a few times on your heels and you will see how. It takes you a much longer time to spin round than the top requires, because you are so much larger than the top. And the earth is so huge that it cannot rotate, or spin round, in less than twenty-four hours, a whole day and night. As there are 365 days in a year the earth turns quite round 365 times while she is moving round the sun, as you might turn round ten times while moving across the room.

Have you ever wondered why it is we have

bright day to work and play in, and then dark night to rest in, and that these never fail to come, the one after the other?

Our earth, without the sun, would be quite dark and cold. Every ray of light, every ray of heat, comes from the sun. And that is why the earth is made always to journey round the sun, and never to wander away; for what could she do out in the cold and the dark?

But the earth is round, the shape of an orange. Some evening, hold an orange close to a candle, and you will see exactly half the orange made bright with the light. The other part is in the shade, and there is a clear though faint line between the light part and the dark part. Do the same thing with a very large ball and the light and dark parts will show more clearly. Hold any round object before a light, and half the object will be lighted up; the other half will remain dark.

The earth is a round object; the sun is its light. Is one half of the world bright, beautiful, and warm; and the other half always dark and cold and dreary, without moving creature or growing plant? No! and the reason of this you can easily prove.

Run a knitting needle through your orange, and turn the orange very slowly round on the needle before the candle. Half is always in the light; half, in the shade. But it is not always the same half. One bit after another gets into the light; what was in the light goes into the shade. Thus every bit of the orange by turns is in the light half, and every bit has its turn in the dark.

Now you see what a beautiful, kind contrivance it is to keep the earth continually turning round before the sun, while she travels round him. By far the greatest part of the earth, all the way round, has its turn in the light and its turn in the dark in twenty-four hours. It is because it takes the earth that time to turn completely round that our day and night last twenty-four hours. The half turned to the sun has day; the half turned from the sun has night. When it is night with us, the people on the opposite half have day, and when we are about our work, they are in bed. This movement of the earth is called its *diurnal* motion. Diurnal means daily; motion is movement.

LESSON X.

THE BLIND BOY.

O say what is that thing call'd light,
  Which I must ne'er enjoy;
What are the blessings of the sight:
  O tell your poor blind boy!

You talk of wondrous things you see;
  You say the sun shines bright;
I feel him warm, but how can he,
  Or make it day or night?

My day or night myself I make
  Whene'er I sleep or play;
And could I ever keep awake
  With me 'twere always day.

With heavy sighs I often hear
  You mourn my hapless woe;
But sure with patience I can bear
  A loss I ne'er can know.

Then let not what I cannot have
  My cheer of mind destroy:
Whilst thus I sing, I am a king,
  Although a poor blind boy.

C. CIBBER.

LESSON XI.

POLES AND AXIS.

IF you watch a wheel turning round quickly,
you will see that the middle part, which is
called the axle, is quite still. When a top is
spinning its fastest, sleeping, as boys say,
the very middle of the top, right through,
down to the point, is still. So, if you could
spin round quickly on your heels, you might
imagine a line through the middle of you,
from your head to your heels, upon which you
spin. That middle line would be still while
all the rest of you was in motion; just as the
knitting needle was still when you turned the
orange round on it.

Everything which turns round or rotates in
this way turns on a still middle line; not a
real line; the stillness is real, but the line is
only imaginary. Such a line is called an
axis. If you could turn round upon your
heels, you would turn upon an axis. The top
spins upon its axis. The earth spins or
rotates upon her axis once in twenty-four
hours. You remember that the earth is a

little flattened at the top and bottom; the axis
runs between the two flattened parts. The
places where the axis would come out if it
were a real, instead of an imaginary, line,
are called poles. Your poles would be, one at
the top of your head, the other at your heels.

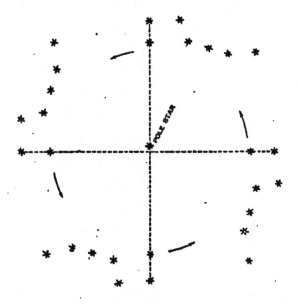

The earth's poles are at the two flattened parts.
One of the poles always points to a particular
star in the heavens called the pole star, and
that is the north pole of the earth; the pole
at the other flattened end is the south pole.

As the ends of the earth, where the poles

are, are slightly flattened, the middle between
the poles bulges out a little, as you may have
seen an orange bulge in the middle.   Round
this bulging middle, exactly between the two

poles, there is another
imaginary line called
the *equator*, because it
divides the earth into
equal parts, and for
another   reason   also.
The equator helps us
to know where places
are, and you will find it
marked upon all maps
of the world.   Sphere,
as you know, is a name given to the earth
because it is a round object; the word *hemi*
means half; so half of the earth is a *hemisphere*.

The equator divides the earth into two
hemispheres or half spheres, as you might
divide an orange into two hemispheres by
tying a string round the middle.   The half
between the equator and the north pole is the
northern hemisphere: the other half, between
the equator and the south pole, is the southern
hemisphere.

Questions on Lessons IX. and XI.

1. What is the earth's axis?—An imaginary line upon which the earth turns round or rotates.

2. Where is this line?—*Through* the middle of the earth, between the two flattened parts.

3. What are the poles?—The two ends of the axis, north and south.

4. In what time does the earth turn quite round? —In a day and night, that is, in twenty-four hours.

5. When have we day?—When our part of the world is turned to the sun.

6. When have we night?—When our part of the world has rolled round, from the sun.

7. What causes the change of day and night?— The rotation of the earth before the sun.

8. What is the equator?—An imaginary line *round* the middle of the earth between the two poles.

LESSON XII.

THE FOUR SEASONS.

PART I.

THE days of our year do not follow, day after day alike, all the year round. We have winter frost and snow, and leafless trees; then,

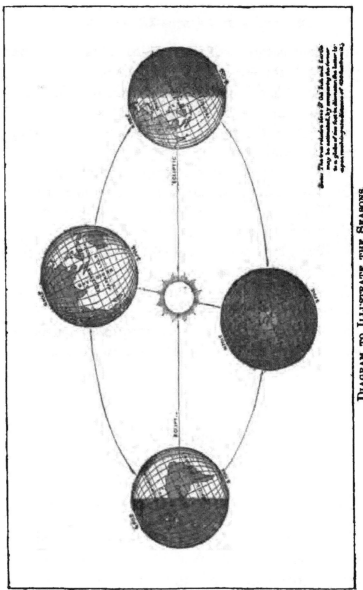

DIAGRAM TO ILLUSTRATE THE SEASONS.

spring; after that, the bright hot summer; next autumn; and then winter again.

We have sunshine in winter as well as in summer, but the two are very different. The summer sun makes us so warm that we can hardly bear our clothes, but in winter we want warm wraps on the brightest day. The reason is, that, though the earth goes on her regular path, and does not go away from the sun, yet our country and others north of the equator are leaning away from him in the winter and towards him in the summer. We live in the northern half of the world, or the northern hemisphere; and this whole hemisphere gets far less sunshine in our winter than in our summer.

How can part of the earth be turned from the sun if the whole earth is not? That is another wonderful, beautiful arrangement God has made, so that nearly all the world should be pleasant to live in. If the earth were to go round the sun with her axis upright, that is, standing up straight from pole to pole, the middle bulging part, where the equator is, would be always just opposite to the sun and would get too much heat. While we, who live a good deal to the north of the equator, should never get enough sunshine to ripen our corn and fruit. The sun's rays would fall straight down upon the equator, and would slope so much to reach us that we should get very little heat. You know it is much warmer in front of a kitchen fire, where the heat comes out straight, than it is in a corner which only slanting rays of heat can reach.

But the earth does not travel with its axis upright. It is always a sloping line; sloping, not toward the sun, but towards the path which the earth travels along; and therefore at one time our north pole is turned towards the sun, and at another time the south pole. Of course there is no real path, it is merely a way through space. But imagine it a real road for a moment, and you can think of the earth bowling along with her axis sloping towards the road.

THE VOICE OF SPRING.

I AM coming, little maiden !
With the pleasant sunshine laden ;
With the honey for the bee ;
With the blossom for the tree ;
With the flower and with the leaf ;
Till I come the time is brief.

I am coming, I am coming !
Hark, the little bee is humming ;
See, the lark is soaring high
In the bright and sunny sky ;
And the gnats are on the wing ;
Little maiden, now is spring !

See the yellow catkins cover
All the slender willows over ;
And on mossy banks so green
Star-like primroses are seen ;
Every little stream is bright ;
All the orchard trees are white.

Hark ! the little lambs are bleating ;
And the cawing rooks are meeting
In the elms,—a noisy crowd ;
And all birds are singing loud ;
And the first white butterfly
In the sun goes flitting by.

MARY HOWITT.

D

LESSON XIV.

THE FOUR SEASONS.

PART II.

THAT is how the earth moves, never turning out of her way, or changing her position in the least, but with her north pole always pointing towards the pole star in the heavens.

Hold a doll sloping towards a table on which a candle is standing. Fix on a bright nail in the room for your *pole star*, and take care always to keep the doll's face looking towards it. Then, carry the doll steadily round the candle, never changing its position, but keeping it always sloping a little towards the table, from the head to the feet. At one time, the candle shines straight on the middle of the doll. Then, move the figure round, always in the same position, and you will find the feet turned towards the candle, and the head turned a little away. Go on still farther; the candle shines again straight on the middle, and neither head nor feet are turned towards it. Go farther round and you will see the head turned towards the light and the feet away. When you get to the point where you began, the candle will again shine upon the middle.

It is rather difficult to keep the doll steady in the same position and always facing the pole star; but if you can manage it you will be able to understand a little how we get the four seasons.

Take an orange, then, instead of the doll, with a line round the middle for the equator, and a knitting needle put through to show where the poles should be. Put an N. at the top for the north pole, and an S. at the bottom for the south pole. Then, carry it gently round the candle with the knitting needle always sloping *a little* towards the table, and the north pole *always pointing to the pole star.* You will find that at one time the north pole turns a little towards the candle, and the south pole a little away. As you go on, the candle shines full on the equator and neither of the poles turns towards it. Go on farther, and the south pole turns to, and the north pole away from the light. Continue moving round, and again the candle shines full on the equator, and neither pole turns towards it.

We live in the northern hemisphere, about halfway between the north pole and the equator. Our warmest time, our summer, is, therefore, when the north pole turns towards the sun. Our coldest time is when the south pole is turned toward, and our part of the world a little away from, the sun, so as to get only his slanting rays. We have our spring and autumn when the sun shines straight down on the equator, and we neither turn toward nor from him. Our autumn is warmer than our spring because the sun has been shining upon us all the summer, and has made our part of the world warm. Just in the same way, a room is made warm that has had a good fire burning in it all day.

As the middle of the earth, about the equator, is the part always nearest to the sun, and is never turned from him, that is the hottest part of the world and it has not the change of the four seasons as we have.

Questions on Lesson XIV.

1. Name the four seasons.—Spring, summer, autumn, winter.

2. What is the difference between them?—Summer is rather hot, winter cold; spring and autumn neither very hot nor very cold.

3. How do we get summer?—Our part of the world, the northern hemisphere, is turned towards the sun, and, therefore, receives much heat.

4. When have we winter?—When the northern hemisphere is turned from the sun.

5. What part of the world is turned to him then? —The southern hemisphere; there they have summer during our winter.

6. When have we spring and autumn?—When the sun shines straight on the equator, and neither of the poles is turned towards him.

LESSON XV.

SUMMER.

" THE flowers are blooming everywhere,
    On every hill and dell;
And oh! how beautiful they are,
    How sweetly, too, they smell!

"The little birds they dance along,
　And look so glad and gay,
I love to hear their pleasant song,
　I feel as glad as they.

"The young lambs bleat and frisk about,
　The bees hum round their hive,
The butterflies are coming out;
　'Tis good to be alive.

"The trees, that looked so stiff and grey,
　With green leaves now are hung;
Oh! mother, let me laugh and play,
　I cannot hold my tongue.

"See yonder bird spreads out its wings,
　And mounts the clear blue skies;
And, hark! how merrily he sings,
　As far away he flies."

"Go forth, my child! and laugh and play—
　And let thy cheerful voice,
With birds, and brooks, and merry May,
　Cry out, 'Rejoice! rejoice!'

"I would not check thy bounding mirth,
　My happy little boy;
For He who made this blooming earth,
　Smiles on an infant's joy."

GILMAN.

LESSON XVI.

HARVEST THANKSGIVING.

PRAISE, O praise our God and King,
Hymns of gladness let us sing,
 For His mercies still endure,
 Ever faithful, ever sure.

Praise Him that He made the sun,
Day by day his course to run,
 For His mercies still endure,
 Ever faithful, ever sure.

And the silver moon by night,
Shining with her gentle light,
 For His mercies still endure,
 Ever faithful, ever sure.

Praise Him that He gave the rain
To make big the swelling grain,
 For His mercies still endure,
 Ever faithful, ever sure:

And hath bid the fruitful field
Crops of yellow grain to yield;
 For His mercies still endure,
 Ever faithful, ever sure.

Praise Him for our harvest-store;
He hath fill'd the garner-floor;
    For His mercies still endure,
    Ever faithful, ever sure.
SIR HENRY BAKER.

LESSON XVII.

WINTER.

WHEN icicles hang by the wall,
  And Dick the shepherd blows his nail,
And Tom bears logs into the hall,
  And milk comes frozen home in pail;
When blood is nipt, and ways be foul,
Then nightly sings the staring owl
        Tu-whoo!
  Tu-whit! tu-whoo! a merry note!
  While greasy Joan doth keel the pot.

When all around the wind doth blow,
  And coughing drowns the parson's saw,
And birds sit brooding in the snow,
  And Marian's nose looks red and raw;
When roasted crabs hiss in the bowl—
Then nightly sings the staring owl
        Tu-whoo!
  Tu-whit! tu-whoo! a merry note!
  While greasy Joan doth keel the pot.
SHAKESPEARE.

LESSON XVIII.

HOT COUNTRIES AND COLD COUNTRIES.

PART I.

THOUGH at one time of the year the north pole is turned a little towards the sun, and at another, the south pole, yet the earth's axis never slants so much as to turn away the broad middle part, where the equator is, from the sun's rays. That middle band of the earth, at the equator and north and south of it, is always the hottest part because it is nearest the sun, and his rays fall upon it straight, and not sloping. Therefore in this part there is no winter cold nor summer heat, no seasons like ours, but hot weather all the year through. Here are the hot countries, where the people with dark skins live, and the palm trees grow; where there are beautiful flowers of every colour, and large juicy fruits; where the feathers of the birds are crimson and purple and gold and green; and where huge wild beasts, both fierce and gentle, roam about in the forests.

This part of the earth's surface is called the

torrid zone, or belt; the word "torrid" means burning, and it is easy to see why the name is suitable. These hot countries are also spoken of as within the tropics. You cannot understand yet what is meant by the "tropics"; but you may remember that the hot countries are tropical, or within the tropics.

An Arctic Scene.

From the equator up towards the north pole the world becomes colder and colder the farther we go, until at last, near the pole, there is perpetual ice and snow. Many ships, manned with brave sailors, have tried to reach the north pole, but they have never been able to get across the frozen seas. No green things grow on these frost-bound lands; there are few living creatures, and huge masses of ice, called icebergs, larger than whole rows of houses, float about where the sea is not altogether frozen. Sad it is for any unfortunate ship which is trying to make way amongst these!

This dreary part of the world is called the frigid, or cold zone, and well deserves its name. Even when the north pole is turned towards the sun there is never enough sunshine to melt the ice. But that part of the year is the summer time in those regions, as with ourselves, and, for the people who live near the pole, is a joyful time for more reasons than one.

LESSON XIX.

THE HUMMING-BIRD.

THE humming-bird! the humming-bird!
  So fairy-like and bright,
It lives among the sunny flowers,
  A creature of delight!

In the radiant islands of the East,
  Where fragrant spices grow,
A thousand, thousand humming-birds
  Go glancing to and fro.

Like living fires they flit about,
  Scarce larger than a bee,
Among the broad palmetto leaves
  And through the fan-palm tree.

And in those wild and verdant woods,
  Where stately mosses tower,
Where hangs from branching tree to tree
  The scarlet passion-flower,—

There builds her nest the humming-bird,
  Within the ancient wood—
Her nest of silky cotton down—
  And rears her tiny brood.

All crimson is her shining breast,
  Like to the red, red rose;
Her wing is the changeful green and blue
  That the neck of the peacock shows.

.Thou happy, happy humming-bird,
  No winter round thee lours,
Thou never saw'st a leafless tree,
  Nor land without sweet flowers.

MARY HOWITT.

LESSON XX.

HOT COUNTRIES AND COLD COUNTRIES.

PART II.

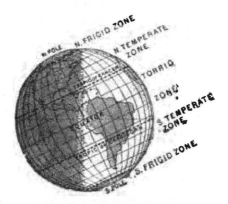

As the earth is round, only half of it can
be lighted at one time by the sun. When
the north pole is turned towards the sun, the
sunlight cannot reach all the way down to the
south pole. It reaches to the north pole,
and falls a good bit over to the other side.

At the time of year when this is the case, there is never any night at the north pole. Though that part of the earth turns round with the rest once in twenty-four hours, yet, as the whole of it is turned towards the sun while the earth rotates, that region " cannot get out of the light"; so there is a long, long summer day up there; and the sun shines in the sky at midnight when we are all in bed and asleep. The nearer we get to the pole, the longer the days become, until at the pole itself there is a single day which lasts for half the year; that is, the sun can be seen all that time.

That is the happy time of the year for the few people who live in these frozen regions. In our winter, it is the south pole which has the sunshine and our north pole is turned away. Then the north pole has a long night, and the people in the frigid zone have to live for months without daylight. When at last the sun rises, it is a great festival, and the people come out of their huts and watch for hours for the joyful sight, which we might see every morning if we were not fast asleep. This is at a long distance from the pole; quite close to the north pole no one can live because there is nothing to eat.

All about the south pole are icebergs, and frozen seas. Here too are long, long days and nights, just as about the north pole. It is another frigid zone. But the south pole has its dark cold winter night when the north pole has its long day, because when the one pole is turned towards the sun, the other is turned away.

Between these two frigid zones and the torrid zone are two broad belts of land, where it is neither very hot nor very cold, and where the people enjoy the pleasant change of the four seasons in their year.

Apples, plums, and corn, and many other things grow in these regions; the fields are green; and the trees lose their leaves in the autumn and get new ones in the spring. These are the temperate zones. That between the torrid zone and the north frigid, is the north temperate zone, in which our own country lies. That between the torrid zone and the south frigid, is the south temperate zone. These broad belts get warmer the nearer we go to the equator, and colder the nearer we draw to the poles. But as the lands in them are never very warm nor very cold, the word *temperate* is used to describe the whole.

When you see a map of the world, you will be able to decide at once whether any land is warm, or cold, or temperate, by considering how far it lies from the equator.

Questions on Lesson XX.

1. Which is the hottest part of the earth?—The Torrid Zone; at the equator and on each side of it.

2. Why?—It is the part nearest the sun, and that upon which his straight rays fall.

3. Which are the coldest parts?—The two Frigid, or Freezing, Zones, one round each pole.

4. Why are these cold?—They are far from the sun, and are warmed only by his slanting rays.

5. What are the belts of the earth between these called?—The North Temperate Zone, and the South Temperate Zone.

6. What can you say about the lands in these?—They have four seasons in their year, and are neither very hot nor very cold.

LESSON XXI.

THE LAND OF ICE AT THE SOUTH POLE.

THE ship drove fast, loud roared the blast,
And southward aye we fled.

And now there came both mist and snow,
And it grew wondrous cold :
And ice, mast high, came floating by,
As green as emerald.

And through the drifts the snowy clifts
Did send a dismal sheen :
Nor shapes of men nor beasts we ken—
The ice was all between.

The ice was here, the ice was there,
The ice was all around :
It cracked and growled, and roared and howled,
Like noises in a swound.

COLERIDGE.

LESSON XXII.

PARALLEL LINES.

IT is very important to know the distance of
places from the equator, because the climate
of a place depends very much upon how far it
is from the equator.

E

Distance from the equator is called *latitude*. Places north of that line are in north latitude; those south of it are in south latitude. But

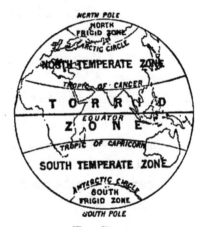

THE ZONES.

it is not enough to know that a place is in north latitude. If you wish to know its climate, and, therefore, what sort of animals live in it, and what plants grow, you must know exactly how far it is from the equator.

That people may know this, other imaginary lines are drawn on maps as if they passed round the earth in the same direction as the equator, and parallel with it. The two rails upon which a tramway or a railway carriage run are parallel; that is, they both run in the same direction, and are always at the same distance from one another.

These imaginary lines round the world, at equal distances from the equator and from each other, are called parallels of latitude, and are marked in maps of the world, or of any part of it.

If you know which parallel a place is upon, you know its distance from the equator, and can judge fairly well how hot or how cold it is. But how are we to know any particular parallel so as to speak of it? Has each a name of its own? Not a name, but a number.

The world is round, and, therefore, any line which goes right round it must be a circle, the shape of a ring. Wise men have divided the circle into 360 equal parts, and each of these parts is called a degree. Divide a circle into quarters, and in each quarter there will be ninety degrees, because four times ninety are 360. A circle drawn round the world from pole to pole, and passing through the equator, must have 360 degrees. From the equator to either of the poles, a quarter of a circle, the distance is ninety degrees.

Imagine a line for each one of these degrees, to measure them off, as the inches are measured off on a foot-rule. These lines must go round the earth, for the measure is wanted everywhere; they must be parallel with the equator, or the measure would not be true. These are parallels of latitude; there are ninety between the equator and the north pole, one for each degree. Between the equator and the south pole there is the same number of parallels of latitude.

A place on the fifth parallel to the north is five degrees north of the equator, and must be hot. A place on the fiftieth parallel is fifty degrees north of the equator, and is temperate, getting rather cold. A place seventy-five degrees north is in the frigid zone, very cold.

These parallels are marked on maps of the world. Each parallel is not always marked; every fifth or tenth is enough to enable us to find a place when once we know that it is so many degrees north or south of the equator. To write that a place is forty-five degrees north latitude, we write 45° N. lat. The little cypher after 45 stands for degrees.

At a distance of $23\frac{1}{2}°$ from the equator, on

each side, are two parallels called *tropics.*
All lands within that space are very hot
and belong to the torrid zone. If you can
remember this you will find it a great help.
You will know that lands 15° N. lat., 10° S.
lat., and so on, are hot lands. Then, if you
could also recollect that at 66½°, north and
south, the frigid zones begin, beyond which
all is generally cold and dreary, you would
have some idea what the climate of places
would be in different parts of the world.

Questions on Lesson XXII.

1. What is latitude?—Distance from the equator,
north or south.

2. Why is it important to know the distance of a
place from the equator?—Because the climate of
the place depends very much upon that.

3. How is latitude measured?—By imaginary lines
round the earth, parallel with the equator.

4. What does "parallel with the equator" mean?
—Running in the same direction as the equator, and
keeping at the same distance from it all the way.

5. How many parallels are there north of the
equator?—Ninety, but they are not all marked on
maps of the world.

6. Which are the most important lines to remember?—Those at 23½° and at 66½° north and
south of the equator.

LESSON XXIII.

DAY-BREAK.

SEE the day begins to break,
And the light shoots like a streak
Of subtle fire; the wind blows cold
While the morning doth unfold;
Now the birds begin to rouse,
And the squirrel from the boughs
Leaps, to get him nuts and fruit,
The early lark, that erst was mute,
Carols to the rising day
Many a note and many a lay.

Shepherds, rise, and shake off sleep—
See the blushing morn doth peep
Through the windows, while the sun
To the mountain-tops is run,
Gilding all the vales below
With his rising flames, which grow
Greater by his climbing still.—
Up! ye lazy swains! and fill
Bag and bottle for the field;
Clasp your cloaks fast, lest they yield
To the bitter north-east wind.
Call the maidens up, and find
Who lies longest, that she may
Be chidden for untimed delay.
Feed your faithful dogs, and pray
Heaven to keep you from decay;
So unfold, and then away.—FLETCHER.

LESSON XXIV.

SUNRISE AND SUNSET.

ONE change which is constantly taking place in the heavens you have no doubt noticed. The sun never seems to remain still in the same place. Every morning, long before you are awake in the summer, but later in the winter, a grand sight is to be seen in the heavens; that is, if the morning should not be cloudy.

At first, there is no sun to be seen, but everything stands out in a clear light, and you know the sun is coming. Then, a certain part of the sky becomes rosy and bright, getting more beautiful and golden every moment. Perhaps there are little lovely pink clouds, or, purple clouds with golden edges floating about. Then you just see a bright golden rim, too dazzling for you to look at, coming up from behind the earth into the golden sky. The rim rises, and rises, until at last the whole round, glorious sun is shining in the sky, which he made so splendid with his rays before he appeared. As the morning goes on, he gets higher and higher in the heavens, and is no longer bathed in golden sky and rosy clouds.

By noon he reaches his highest point, nearly overhead; and he still continues his course across the sky, until, in the evening, he reaches the point just opposite to that where his course began.

Then he gradually goes down with the same splendour with which he rose;—sometimes in a sky which looks like a great sea of gold with cities and palaces and all beautiful forms rising out of it. After the last edge of the sun has disappeared below the earth, a clear soft light remains for a while, such as came before his rising in the morning: this is called *twilight*.

The sun rises in the *east* and sets in the *west*. By remembering this, you will be able to tell the direction in which the places near your own town, or the streets of your own town, lie.

Stand so that your right hand is towards the east where the sun rises, your left towards the west, where the sun sets. Then you are looking towards the north pole and your back is towards the south pole. All the houses, streets, and towns on your right hand side are to the east of you; those on your left are to the west of you.   The places you must walk straightforward to reach, are north, and the places behind you are to the south.

If you are in a place new to you, where you have never seen the sun rise or set, and want to know in what direction a certain road runs, you must notice in what direction your own shadow falls at twelve o'clock.   At noon, the shadows of all objects fall towards the north. Then if you face the north, you have, as before, the south behind you, the east on your right hand, and the west on your left.   Or, if you face the sun at noon, you face south.

When people are moving from place to place, it is important that they should know if they are going southward or northward. In our own country, which is in north latitude, the farther north we go, the colder it becomes; and the warmest part of England lies quite to the south.   The railways on which we travel from place to place are called the "Great Northern," "Great Eastern," "South Western," or "Great Western," according to the direction in which they run.

People like to know, also, where the wind comes from, as that enables them to judge what kind of weather may be expected. If it be from the north, "The north wind doth blow, and we shall have snow"; if it blow from the west, a west wind, we expect rain.

You may get very ready in noticing the directions of places by a little practice. Notice how each of the windows of your school faces, or each of the rooms in your home; the rows of houses you pass on your way to school: and which are the north, south, east, and west sides of churches. The direction of places, the way buildings look, and the way the wind blows, are among the things that intelligent people like to know.

Questions on Lesson XXIV.

1. Where does the sun rise?—In the east.
2. Where does he set?—In the west.
3. If you stand with your right hand to the east, in which direction are you looking?—To the north.
4. Where is the south?—Opposite to the north.

5. How may you find out the direction you are moving in at noon?—Look at our own shadow, it points north.

6. How may the other points be known?—If we stand as before, facing the north, the south is behind us, the east to the right hand, and the west to the left.

LESSON XXV.

EVENING.

SHEPHERDS all, and maidens fair,
Fold your flocks up, for the air
'Gins to thicken, and the sun
Already his great course has run.
See the dew drops how they kiss
Every little flower that is,
Hanging on their velvet heads,
Like a rope of crystal beads.
See the heavy clouds low falling,
And bright Hesperus down calling
The dead night from underground.

FLETCHER.

LESSON XXVI.

WHY THE SUN RISES AND SETS.

THIS appearance of the sun going over our earth every day was very puzzling to the ancients. Their first idea was that the sun travelled round our world every day—going round it like a huge lamp and thus lighting up part after part. But the great sun is many thousand times larger than our little earth. Also, it is very far away, and, therefore, would have to travel a very long distance to get round the earth. As this journey could not be finished in twenty-four hours, it is plain that the change of day and night must be caused in some other way.

If a person be carried along in a railway carriage at a very quick rate, he does not seem to be moving at all himself, but houses, trees, and towns, seem to be running fast in the opposite direction. So, if you turn round quickly, the room seems to be spinning round fast the other way. In the same way, the sun appears to take his daily course over the earth, moving from east to west, while it is really the earth which moves in quite the opposite direction—from west to east. The sun, at least as far as we are concerned, is standing still.

The earth, as you know, is constantly turning round before the sun; half is always in the light of the sun, and half in the dark. But as the earth is always turning, part after part comes up under the sun, and part after part goes down into the shade.

In our early morning, the part of the earth we live upon, England, gradually rolls round towards the sun. First we see a little rim of him in the distance, but the roundness of the earth comes between us and the whole sun. Then we go rolling on towards the sun, until we see the whole of him. We still roll forward, till we get under the sun and have him nearly overhead. Then it is twelve o'clock, or noon, not only with us, but with all the places and people just in a line with us, north and south.

All these places have rolled under the sun just at the same moment as ourselves. You will understand this if you will draw chalk lines between the two flattened ends of an

orange, and then twirl it slowly between your
thumb and finger. You will find that the
whole of one line comes forward at once;
 then the whole of the next,
and so on, just as all the
places in a line from pole to
pole come forward at once as
the earth turns.

As the earth goes on rolling, our country is no longer
nearly under the sun as at
mid-day, but rolls farther and farther back,
until we begin to lose sight of him. At last
we turn right away, and get not one ray of
his light, not even the twilight which lasts
for a little while after the sun has set.

Then it is our night; but though we have
turned away, all the world is not dark. The
part opposite to our feet, on the other side
of our round earth, has rolled full into the
sunshine, and when it is midnight with us,
there the sun is overhead and it is noon.

LESSON XXVII.

MID-DAY LINES.

SUCH lines as we have imagined between the flattened ends of an orange to join together the parts that roll into the light at the same time, are supposed to be drawn from pole to pole on the earth's surface, passing through the equator.

Each of these lines passes through all the places that have their noon, or mid-day, at the same time. It is noon at any place because that part of the earth has rolled forward so as to come under the sun. As the whole earth from north to south rolls forward at once, all places exactly north or south of one another have mid-day at the same moment. The imaginary lines passing through such places are called *meridians*. The word meridian means mid-day, and meridians are mid-day lines. They are the lines marked on globes and maps running from north to south.

These meridian lines are of great use, as they enable us to judge how far places are from each other, east and west. By means of

the equator and the lines which run parallel
with it, we know how far north or south of
the equator any place lies. But we might
search all round the globe before we found a
place a certain number of degrees north of the
equator, if we did not know which meridian
line went through it.

We English people number the meridian
lines from Greenwich, a place near London.

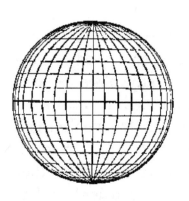

The line which runs
from pole to pole and
passes through Green-
wich is the first me-
ridian. Every place
exactly north and
south of Greenwich,
all the way to the
poles, has the first
meridian passing through it, and has noon at
the same time as ourselves. There is a
meridian line to measure off every degree
upon the equator, though they are not always
all marked upon maps. The distance between
places east and west, is called *longitude*.

All parts of the world that lie to the east of
Greenwich are in east longitude. The rest of

the world, the half that lies to the west of Greenwich, is in west longitude. The meridians are marked 2° W. or 25° W., according to the number of degrees they are west of Greenwich; or, 50° E. long., if they lie so far to the east of Greenwich. Places east of Greenwich, or in east longitude, have their noon before we do, because they turn towards the sun in the morning before we do. All places in west longitude have their noon later.

If a sailor knows that a place is so many degrees to the north of the equator, and so many degrees to the east of Greenwich, he knows exactly where to look for it. How he is able to guide his ship to the very point he wants to reach, you will learn in your next lesson.

Questions on Lessons XXVI. and XXVII.

1. What is a meridian?—An imaginary line, from pole to pole, passing through the equator.

2. What does the word "meridian" mean?—Midday.

3. Why are the meridians so called?—Because they pass through all places that have mid-day at the same time.

4. Why do places north and south of each other

F

have mid-day at the same time?—Because each portion of the earth, from pole to pole, turns towards the sun at the same time.

5. How many of these meridians are there ?—360 ; one through each degree on the circle of the equator.

6. Which is our first meridian ?—The one running through Greenwich.

7. What is the distance of places from Greenwich, east and west, called ?—East and west longitude.

8. What is the great use of these lines?—They enable us to know the distance of all places from Greenwich, east or west.

LESSON XXVIII.

THE POINTS OF THE COMPASS.

PERHAPS you have seen a compass, and have been delighted with the wonderful needle which seems to move about of its own accord, as if it were alive.

The needle is enclosed in a round box. At the bottom of the box is a card marked, as in the picture, with many points, each pointing to certain letters within a circle. Beyond this are numbers, dividing the circles into degrees, ninety in each quarter. The four points most clearly marked are N., S., E.,

and W., that is, north and south, opposite to
each other, and east and west, also opposite.
These four are the cardinal points of the
compass; cardinal, because they are the chief
or principal points.

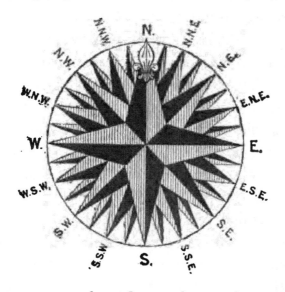

Between north and east is a point marked
N.E., north-east, the direction which is midway between north and east. There are six
other points between north and east, the
names of which you need not learn at present.
Each of the other quarters is divided in the
same way, as you will see in the figure. The
compass has thirty-two points in all. The

F 2

four cardinal points, and the four points exactly between these, are the most important, and are all you need remember.

Poised in the middle of the box, so that it does not touch either the card or the lid, but can swing round easily, is what is called the *needle,* a slight bar of steel, pointed at each end.

Hold the N. of the compass towards the north. Then, with the compass in your hand turn towards the east, and you will see a remarkable thing. The little needle moves, too, but moves quite by itself in just the other direction. Turn to the west, and again the needle moves in the opposite direction to that in which you move. However little you turn a little quiver of the needle follows your movement. And you look at it, wondering how the little thing could perceive you had moved when you hardly knew it yourself. Walk straight on in any direction, and the needle is fairly steady; only fairly steady, because you are sure, without intending it, to move a little to the right or the left.

Turn round very slowly, a little bit at a time, beginning at the north and turning towards the east, and you may make the

needle also move round in a circle. It moves
in the opposite direction to yourself, for it is
trying to get back to the north from which
you are turning.

Suppose that a line were drawn round you,
a yard off, as you turn, by the time you face
the north again the line would be a circle,
and might be divided into quarters, with 90°
in each, like the circle upon the card of the
compass. It might also have letters, N., S.,
W., E., within it showing each direction in
which you faced as you turned slowly round.
If the line, instead of being close to you, were
as far off as the eye could reach, it would still
be a circle.

This distant circle where the earth and
sky seem to meet, is, as you know, the line of
the horizon. The circle upon the card of the
compass, divided into degrees, represents the
circle of the horizon; with the points north,
east, south, and west marked upon it: and,
whichever way you turn, the needle will
always point to the north.

A little pocket compass, which may be
bought for sixpence or less, would help you
to understand this lesson.

1. How many points of the compass are there?—Thirty-two.

2. Which are the principal?—The four cardinal points; north, south, east, west.

3. Which points are next in importance?—The points in the directions midway between these.

4. Name them?—North-east, south-east, south-west, north-west.

5. What does the circle upon the card of the compass represent?—The circle of the horizon.

6. How is it divided?—Into degrees, like all circles, 90° in each quarter.

LESSON XXIX.

THE MARINER'S COMPASS.

WHY does the needle move at all? When you turn from the north, why does it move the other way?

The little piece of steel which forms the needle of the compass is a *magnet*. When you are older you will probably know more, but at present you can learn one thing about magnets.

Whenever a magnet has free play, it will

not rest until one end of it turns to the north, towards the north pole; the other to the south, towards the south pole.

To be free to turn, the magnet must not lie flat upon a table, but should be hung in a loop of thread fastened round the middle of it, or be placed lightly, as it is in the compass, on a little point called a pivot.

If you consider, you will understand how it is that when you turn from the north the needle moves, not with you, but the other way.

The needle is a magnet; it must point to the north. If you face the north, the needle points in the way you are looking; if you turn to the right the needle flies just as far to the left. If it remained still when you turned, that is, if it allowed itself to be carried round with you, it would point east, not north. You can tell how far you have moved in any direction by noticing how many degrees the needle has to move back to find the north.

If you turn about quickly, you cause the little needle to fly to and fro like a wild thing in a cage in its struggle to point true to the north.

If we lived in waste lands, where there are
no roads or waymarks, a compass would be
very valuable.   By noticing how the needle
pointed as we journeyed away from home, we
should know what direction we ought to take
to find our way home again.   In a country like
England, which has roads and railways leading to every place of any size, a compass is
not much wanted.   But think what a friend
it must be to the sailor on the wide, track-
less sea, where there are no roads, no eastern
or northern railways; where the ships that
have gone the same way before, leave not the
faintest mark; where the seaman finds no
more waymark or sign-post than a bird has
in flying through the air.

Have you ever wondered how it is that a
ship finds its way across seas?   How is it
that if you get into a ship for New York, she
makes her way nearly as direct for New
York as a railway train upon land makes for
London; though the ship certainly has not
two iron rails, leading straight to the place,
to run upon?

Before his ship starts, the captain studies
the map to see exactly how many degrees

N.E. or S.W. of London, let us say, the place to which he is going lies. When he knows what direction he is to take, the compass points out the way to him. It shows him that he is going towards the north-east, or south-west, or to whatever point he wishes to make for, and guides him so surely, that he can sail over the world without ever losing his way. Because it is such a friend to the sailor, this wonderful instrument is called the *Mariner's* compass.

If there were no such instrument, ships would not venture much out of sight of land; for, with nothing to guide them, they would miss their way, or run into unknown dangers.

LESSON XXX.

THE PLAN OF A ROOM.

WE have spoken of a map or picture of the world, and you have perhaps wondered how it is possible to make a picture of so large an object, of which only a very small part can be seen at once.

A map is not really a picture, it is a plan. A picture of a house reminds you of the house. It shows the shape, perhaps the colour, and has the general look of the real object. A plan is also a sort of likeness, more useful than a picture, but it does not remind you of the object it represents.

When we have seen how plans of small places are made, and the uses they serve, you will be better able to understand the meaning of a map.

PLAN OF SCHOOL ROOM

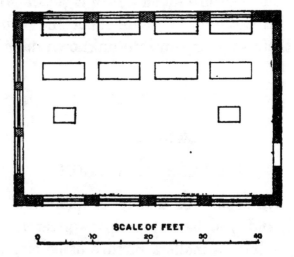

SCALE OF FEET

Here is the plan of the floor of a school-room. You are supposed to be looking at it

from a great height, up above. As you look
from a great distance, everything looks small.
As you look from above, everything appears
to lie flat on the floor. Desks, stools, and
tables seem to have no supports, but to lie
with their tops level with the ground.

So far, it is easy to draw a plan. You
could make one of any room if you imagine
yourself to be looking down from a great
height so that you would see tables and chairs
looking like little flat squares and rounds on
the floor. But such a plan would be of no
use. A plan is only useful when it shows the
exact size as well as shape of the real things;
where they stand, north or south, east or
west; and just how far they are from one
another.

By looking at the plan before us, we learn
that the schoolroom it represents is forty-five
feet long and thirty broad. That the desks
stand against the north wall. That they are
seven and a half feet long, and two and half
feet apart. That the teachers' desks stand out
five feet from those of the scholars. How do
we get such an exact idea of the schoolroom
from this small plan? Notice the little

measure drawn below the plan which is called a *scale*. The scale is divided into lengths, about a quarter of an inch each, and each of these divisions stands for five feet. That is, a quarter of an inch on the scale stands for a length of five feet of the walls and desks of the schoolroom. We compare the scale with the plan of the schoolroom and see that the long walls are as long as nine of these five-foot measures, so we know the room is nine times five, or forty-five feet long; and so on with the other walls and the objects in the room.

To make a plan of a room, you must first make a scale, with a certain measure to stand for five or three or ten feet. It does not matter how many, if you put the number down on the scale. Then observe how the walls of the room lie, north, south, east, west. Take a foot-rule and measure your longest wall. Draw a line as many measures of the scale in length as will stand for the length of the room. Do the same with the shorter wall. Then draw the two opposite walls of the same length. Put letters N.E. or S.W. to show the position of each wall. Then measure the objects in the room, and the distance of each object from the walls, putting each one into your plan, according to the scale.

Now you have an exact plan of the room from which a person who had never seen it could tell its shape, size, aspect, or the way it looks, north or south; what things are in the room, where they stand, and how far they are from one another.

Questions on Lesson XXX.

1. What may be learnt from the plan of a building?—Its exact size and shape, and its aspect, or the direction in which it looks.

2. How is the size shown?—By the scale.

3. What is a scale?—A measure which shows that a certain length in the plan stands for a certain length in the real object.

LESSON XXXI.

THE PLAN OF A TOWN.

SUPPOSE that a lark, who could think, were flying over your town away up in the sky, and paused overhead for a moment to see what there was below him.

He would only see the principal things, streets, and large buildings. Everything would look very small because he would be

PLAN OF A TOWN

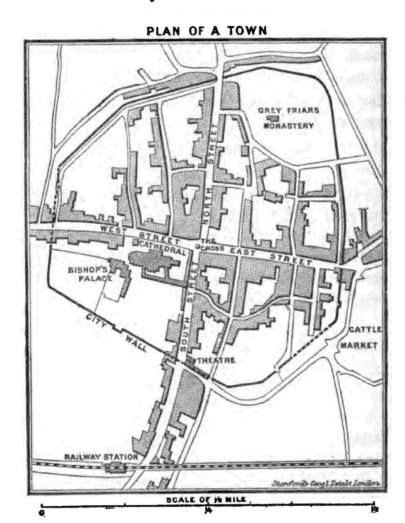

so far off; and as he would see them from above, the buildings would look flat. Such a view of a town is given on the opposite page. It is the old city of Chichester, which is built upon a very simple plan. About the middle of the plan you see a round dot, marked *cross*; that is the beautiful old cross of carved stone which stands in the middle of the city, and from which you may look down the four chief streets. These run in a pretty direct line towards the four cardinal points; *East Street*, towards the east, where the sun rises; *West Street*, towards the west, where he sets; *North Street*, towards the north; and *South Street*, towards the south. There are several smaller streets running out of each of these, and, between the streets, are buildings. The fine old *Cathedral*, which you may enter from West Street or from South Street, is the building for which Chichester is famous; the plan gives you some idea of its shape. At the south-west corner of the cathedral you see the *Bishop's Palace* marked. The city of Chichester has broad old walls—which form a pleasant walk for the towns-folk—nearly all round it.

But a plan must show the distance of the buildings from one another, the length and width of the streets, and the size of the whole town.

Look at the scale below the plan, which stands for half a mile. Each of the four chief streets is about half the length of the scale, or a quarter of a mile, long. South Street, however, is longer than the others, because it goes beyond the city to the station. The length of any of the other streets and the distance between any two buildings you can find out yourself by using the scale.

We can have a plan of a country or a piece of a country as well as of a town or room. Each measure of the scale must stand for a long distance when the plan is of a large place, and for a short distance when the place is small. Thus we can tell the size of a large place from a small plan by looking at the scale.

LESSON XXXII.

MAP OF A COUNTY.

IF it were possible for our bird, flying still higher up in the air, to take a view of the county you live in, as well as of your town, a plan of such a view would be that which is given in what is called a map.

A map would show the chief things in the county :—towns dotted about here and there; perhaps a row or range of hills running across the county, past town after town; a great stream of water, called a river, making its way to the sea, and little streams running along to join the big river: the sea on one side, it may be, running into the land here and there and making curious patterns.

In a map of a county there is no room to mark the streets and buildings of each town. Indeed the town itself is only marked by a dot to show where it is, and its name is written near the dot.

Hills take up a good deal more room than towns, because they generally run over a great piece of country. They are marked on

G

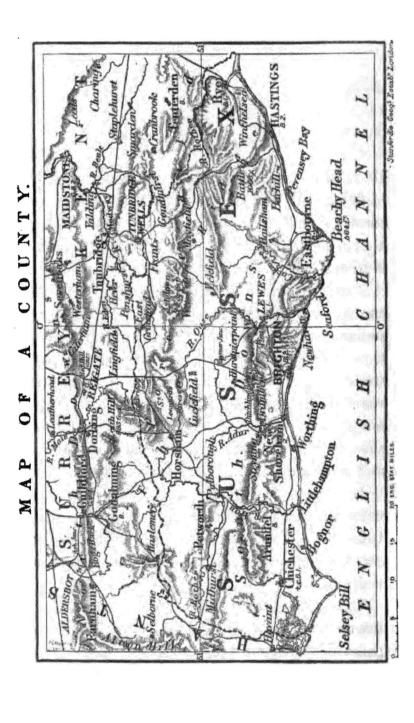

MAP OF A COUNTY.

maps by shaded lines, as when the sun shines
on one side of a hill the other sides look dark
and shady. Rivers are marked by a wavy
line; thick, if the river is wide across; thin,
if it is narrow.

If you wish to draw a map of your own
county, you must first make a scale, as your
map should show how large your county is.
Perhaps each measure of the scale will stand
for ten miles; then, if the county be thirty
miles long and twenty broad, the map will be
three measures long and two broad.

You will next show upon what part of the
earth's surface your county is by putting in
the parallels and meridians. If the 52nd
parallel runs through it, you know it is 52°
north of the equator; if the 2nd meridian,
you know it is two degrees west of Greenwich.

Then you must draw the shape of your
county as accurately as you can. The only
way you can find out the shape, is by copying
it from some other map.

The line showing the north of the county
is to be the top of your drawing; the bottom,
the south; the right hand, the east; the left

hand, the west. Maps are always made with
the north at the top; so, as you look towards
the north or top, you have the east on your
right and the west on your left. The bottom
of the map is the south.

Perhaps a range of hills runs across the
north of your county for twenty miles, which
you will mark by a shaded line two measures
long. Then there may be a little river of
eight, and a long river of thirty miles, winding
in and out till they get to the sea. These go
into the map as wavy lines so many measures
long.

Then come dots for the towns. These are
put north or west as they may lie, and half
a measure, or one or two measures apart
according as they are five or ten or twenty
miles distant from one another. There is no
room on small maps for little villages.

Next put in the names of the counties that
border your county all round; or if it is
bordered on one side by the sea, the name of
the sea.

By looking at the map and scale now it is
finished you can tell several facts about your
own county.

You see its shape. You can find out its size and its distance from the equator. You may name the hill ranges and rivers in it, and say where they run and how long they are. You may name, also, all the towns, and say how far they are from one another, and what direction, north or west, a man must go in to get from one town to another. You see, too, what county you would get into if you went out of yours on the south or east or north side.

Questions on Lesson XXXII.

1. How may the size of a county be learned from a map?—By the scale, which shows that a measure, perhaps half an inch long, stands for ten or twenty miles.

2. How may we know its distance from the equator?—By the parallel which runs through, or near the county. The number of the parallel shows the number of degrees it is from the equator.

3. What does the map teach as to the appearance of a county?—The map shows if it is flat or hilly; if it has many rivers; if the sea washes it, and runs up into the land.

4. What may we learn about the towns?—Where they lie in the county, north, south, or west; and

how far we must go to get from our own town to any other.

5. Does the map show in what part of England our county is?—Yes; it shows what counties border ours on every side; or, if the sea washes the county, the name of the sea.

LESSON XXXIII.

HOW MAPS ARE MADE.

IT is easy enough to make a map from which much may be learned when there is another map to copy it from; but the *first* map of any district, how was that made? How was it possible to make a map of a great piece of land when it is only possible to see a small part at once? There are still some parts of the world about which all that can be written on the map is " Unexplored "; which means that nobody from any civilised land has been there, or knows what those lands are like.

You have learned already that brave men are constantly taking most dangerous journeys to discover these unexplored regions. When a traveller has found out and examined a new

place, his first care is to make a map of it, for
the use of the rest of the world.

First, he measures every mile of the land
carefully, by a method which you cannot
understand. Then, he draws the exact shape

THE WORLD
AS KNOWN IN THE TIME OF CHRIST.

according to scale. Then he measures and
marks down in its right position every hill,
mountain, valley, river, forest, village—whatever, in fact, he finds in this newly-discovered
land. But how can he tell in what part of
the whole world this new land lies? It is

very necessary to know this, and he finds out before he begins to measure or draw.

Persons who have studied these things can always find out what latitude they are in by observing the sun and the stars. That is, they can learn exactly how far they are from the equator. Stranger still, they can find out their longitude, or their distance west or east of Greenwich, by means of a time-piece, or chronometer, which every ship carries.

Now, if they know their exact distance from Greenwich, and their exact distance from the equator, they know exactly whereabouts on the earth's surface they are, and can put their new map into its right place on the old maps of the world. You will be able to understand how the captain of a ship finds out his latitude and longitude in the open sea when you get a little older.

In this careful way, mile by mile, nearly the whole surface of the earth has been measured and mapped out. A map of the world, which you may buy for a penny, was not made at one time and by one person. It has taken three or four hundred years to make, and has been drawn in bit by bit, by one and another, as each found out and mapped out some new land which before his time had been "unexplored." When we think of this we should be ready to give careful heed to the study of maps, the making of which has cost not only much labour, but many noble lives.

As the world is round, the best way to make a map of the whole of it, with all its lands and waters, is on a round globe such as we often see. Such a globe has the equator round the middle, the meridians, running from north to south and meeting at the poles, and the parallel lines round the earth, in the same direction as the equator. But maps of any part of the world are always made flat.

LESSON XXXIV.*

THE SURFACE OF THE EARTH.

PART I.

WHEREVER we go upon our earth we find ourselves upon one of two things; we are

* This and the following lessons should be read with the map of the world.

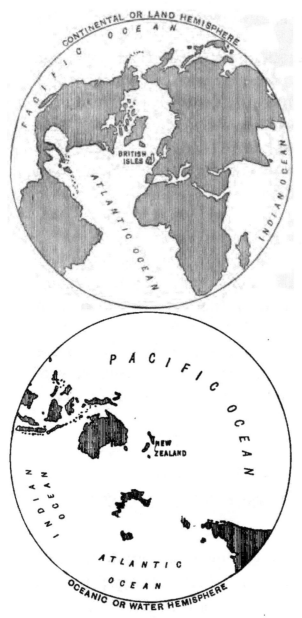

LAND AND WATER HEMISPHERES.

either upon land or upon water. The surface
of the earth consists of land and water. We
say the surface because it is only of the surface or outside of this huge ball, our world,
that we are speaking. But how are the land
and water divided? Does all the land lie
together in one place, and all the water in
another? And which is there the most of,
land or water?

Look at a map of the world: most likely it
is divided into two hemispheres: not northern
and southern, which we have spoken of, but
eastern and western. That is, the earth is
supposed to be divided as an orange would be
if you cut it through the middle between the
two flattened ends, and spread out the outer
skins of each half side by side.

The first thing that strikes you is that
there is a great deal more water than land;
that about three quarters of the earth's surface is covered with water, while only one
quarter is land. Perhaps you expected that
most of the earth's surface would be land, for
men to live upon, and for the plants they
need for food to grow on. Some day you
will understand that men could not live, nor

green things grow on the earth, unless there were far more of what seems waste water than of fertile land.

The water, you will see, runs into the land here and there, and gives it many irregular shapes. Indeed, the shape of the land depends entirely upon the water which borders it.

In the western hemisphere there is a great mass of land, or, rather, there are two great masses joined together, which are something like two legs of mutton in shape; and are called North America and South America.

In the northern of these, or North America, there are four great breaks on the eastern side, made by the sea running in; the southern mass of land, or South America, is nearly unbroken. The two together stretch a great way from north to south between the poles.

There are no more masses of land in the western hemisphere; but there are many small pieces dotted about here and there in the water. There is a great deal of water in the western hemisphere, far more than in the eastern.

LESSON XXXV.

THE SURFACE OF THE EARTH.

PART II.

In the eastern hemisphere the land lies chiefly to the north of the equator; most of the water in this division is south of the equator. There is a great mass of land in the north, stretching from east to west, and broken into in many places by the water.

Joined to this mass by a little narrow neck of land, is another great mass through which the equator passes. South of the equator, is another huge piece of land with water all round it, and many smaller pieces surrounded by the water.

These large divisions of the land are called *continents*. A continent is the largest division of land. The continent in the western hemisphere, which is nearly in two separate pieces, is America, North and South.

The mass of land which stretches from east to west in the eastern hemisphere, though it is really only one continent, has two names,

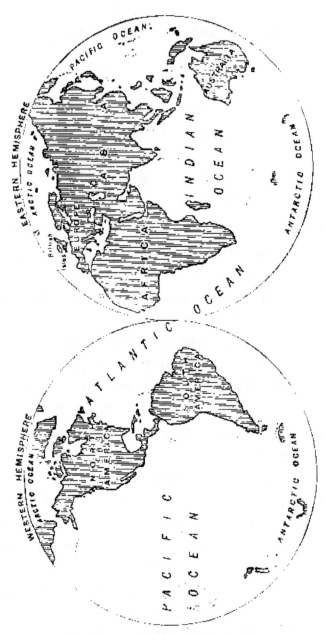

EASTERN AND WESTERN HEMISPHERES.

and is generally spoken of as two. The larger part on the east is Asia, and the smaller division on the west is Europe. Both of these are much broken into by the water, but Europe more so than Asia.

The continent joined to Asia by a little neck of land is Africa, which, like South America, is not much broken by the sea.

The continent south of the equator with water all round it is Australia.

The smaller pieces of land surrounded by water are not called continents, but islands. Australia is sometimes called an island, because it has water all round it.

The part of the land which borders the water is called the coast or the coast line. Those continents into which the water makes its way in many places and for a great distance, have, as you would expect, the most coast or the longest coast line compared with their size.

Questions on Lesson XXXV.

1. What is a continent?—The largest division of land.

2. How many continents are there?—Five.

3. Name them.—Europe, Asia, Africa, America, and Australia.

4. What is the *coast?*—That part of the land which is washed by the sea.

Map Questions.

1. Which continents are upon the equator?

2. Which two continents are north of the equator?

3. Which lies south of the equator?

4. Which is the longest continent from north to south?

5. Name the four continents in the eastern hemisphere.

6. What continent lies east of Europe?

7. What continent lies west of Europe?

8. What continent is to the south of Europe?

9. What continent is quite surrounded by water?

10. What continent would be surrounded by water but for one little neck of land?

LESSON XXXVI.

HIGHLANDS AND LOWLANDS.

Most likely you know the pleasure of being on a hill-top; of the rest, after a long pull up hill, when you look round and see the villages you know dotted about quite small in the distance; and then, of the scamper about with the fresh wind blowing in your face.

Everybody likes the hills; and one reason why England is so pleasant a country is that there are many hills scattered about in it.

A MOUNTAIN CHAIN.

These are not often single hills, but long rows, or *ranges*, as they are called, which run through several counties.

A wide stretch of level country, with no hills worth speaking of, is called a *plain*.

Any rising ground is a hill; but if the ground rise so high that it takes a man some hours' hard climbing to get to the top, it is called a *mountain*. There are mountains in

H

the world so high that the top or *summit* has never been reached; and others, whose sides are so steep that it is impossible to climb them.

Mountains, like hills, do not often stand alone; they are either in ranges or *chains*, or several lie close together in a *group*.

Between two or three mountains, the land dips down into a hollow or *valley*.

Sometimes, at the bottom of a mountain valley, lies a blue *lake*, making a picture in its waters of the sky and clouds above, and of the mountains which tower all round it. Perhaps there are little islands rising here and there above its surface.

Sometimes two or three chains of mountains run side by side, or parallel with each other. When this is the case there are valleys, often many miles wide, between the chains. Most mountains have several *peaks*, often far apart, for a mountain is generally a huge mass many miles round at the *base* or bottom and thinning away into ridges at the top.

After getting up to what looks like the top of a mountain from below, we should in some places find ourselves on a wide open country

like a plain, only that it rises high above the
rest of the land. A large tract which stands
high above the country round, as a table stands
above a floor, is called a *tableland.* Countries
or districts with mountain chains or groups
are said to be mountainous. It is a pleasant
thing to live among mountains; to be in sight
of what is great and beautiful far beyond
anything men can make. You learn to know
the great rugged shapes so well that you can
see them with your eyes shut. You know
how the mountains look at any time of day or
in any kind of weather. For they are always
changing. At one time they are so wrapped
up in clouds that you cannot see them. Again,
they look clear and bright and quite near;
and then, again, they appear far away, and
covered with a soft purple haze. And what
pleasure there is in mountain climbing; which
is always hard work, and often dangerous, but
is so delightful that people travel hundreds of
miles for the pleasure of feeling the clear,
cold mountain air.

Though the heat may be unbearable at the
base or foot of a mountain, the air grows colder
and colder as you rise. At the top, if the

H 2

mountain be lofty, there is nothing but eternal snow, and great fields of ice in the high valleys; snow and ice which do not entirely thaw away in the hottest summer days. Indeed, near the equator, where the lowlands are always hot, the cold is as great on the tops of high mountains as it is at the poles. You cannot at present understand why, but the fact is, if we could rise two or three miles into the air, above our own homes, we should get into a climate as cold as we should find in the frozen oceans. The highest mountains in the world are between five and six miles in height. None of our English mountains are quite one mile above the level of the sea. The height of mountains is always measured from the surface or level of the sea, because, when it is calm, the sea keeps at about the same height all over the world.

Questions on Lesson XXXVI.

1. What is a hill?—Rising ground.

2. What is a mountain?—A mass of ground more than half a mile in height.

3. What is a plain?—A tract of level land.

4. What is a tableland?—A tract of land raised high above the country round it.

5. What is a valley?—Land that sinks or dips below the country about it.

6. Name the parts of a mountain.—The base, or foot; the sides; the peaks; and the summit, or highest point.

7. How do mountains usually lie?—In chains, or ranges; or in groups.

8. What is a chain or range?—Mountains following one another in a row.

9. What is a group?—Several mountains clustered together.

LESSON XXXVII.

RIVERS.

HAVE you ever sent a paper boat floating down a stream? You know how fast it goes; not because the wind blows it, but because the water carries it along. The waters of the stream are moving, running. What you look at this moment, you will never see again, though more water will come, and hasten after that which has gone on. When the shore is reached, the waters pour into the sea, day and night without ceasing.

Most likely the stream does not go to the

sea by itself; it may pour its waters into another larger river; but one way or other, to the sea it goes at last. If you stand on a bridge which goes across a wide river, and

A RIVER.

watch the waters rushing along, fast and strong, and never stopping, you wonder where all the water comes from; and why it is never emptied away, when such great riverfuls are being always poured into the sea. How that is, and how a river begins, and how it grows, and how it is that a river blesses the land it flows through and makes it fertile, are things you will understand when you know more geography. Only think of this now; when you see no wavy river marks upon the map of any country, be sorry for its people; for that is not a land of green fields or forest trees, of corn or fruit.

Rivers have small beginnings; a little stream flows out of a spring of clear, fresh water bubbling up from the ground. Then, other little streams, and larger streams, and at last other rivers join it, until it becomes a broad, deep river, upon which ships can sail. Where does it begin, and how does it find a place to flow in? It begins generally upon high ground, often on mountain sides, but not always; this beginning is called its *source*. The running water wears away the earth and so makes a place for itself; the more water there is, the wider is this channel, which is called the *bed* of the river, because the river lies in it. The land on each side of the river is called a *bank*.

Water spilt upon a table finds its way to the

floor; it is the way of water to get as low down as it can. Therefore rivers make their way to the lowest part of the country they are flowing through. Where you see river lines on a map, you may be sure, that that is the lowest part of the country; that the land rises, a little at least, on each side of the *river valley*.

A LAKE.

Sometimes the river comes to a hollow place in its valley, much wider than itself, and deep like its own bed. It fills up such a hollow with its waters and passes on. This is how most *lakes* are formed. Look at a lake on a map, and you will generally see that a river enters it at one end, and leaves it again at the end nearest the sea.

Rivers which flow into larger rivers are *tributaries.* The *mouth* of a river is where its waters flow into the sea. Sometimes a large river, when near the sea, divides into branches, and has then many mouths; and the land between these branches is called a *delta.*

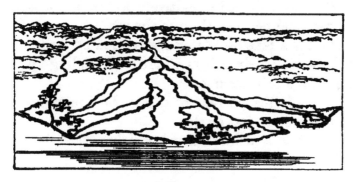

A Delta.

If a river rises in low ground and flows over a plain, its waters move slowly. Mountain rivers have a rapid *current*, their waters flow fast.

Questions on Lesson XXXVII.

1. What is a stream?—Running water.

2. What is a river?—A large stream of fresh water.

3. What is the source of a river?—Its beginning.

4. What is its mouth?—The end of a river, where its waters pour into the sea.

5. What is its bed?—The channel which holds the waters of the river.

6. What are its banks?—The land which borders a river on each side.

7. What is a river valley?—The low land along the bottom of which the river runs.

8. What are tributaries?—Rivers which flow into other rivers and not directly into the sea.

9. What is a lake?—Water surrounded by land.

10. How may a river form a lake?—By filling up a hollow place in its course.

11. What is the current of a river?—The movement of its waters, fast or slow.

12. What is a delta?—Land which a river has formed at its mouth.

LESSON XXXVIII.

COUNTRIES.

WE are English people or English children because our fathers and mothers and their \thers and mothers lived and were born in

MAP OF BRITISH ISLES, with Mountains, Rivers, and Towns.

England. England is our *country*, and Englishmen are our fellow countrymen. Most English people are proud of their country and love it dearly. When they go into foreign lands they like every one to know that they are English. The people of other countries have the same feeling about their native land : everybody thinks his own country is the best and the pleasantest.

Each of the continents contains many countries. The lands or waters which border a country all round are called its *boundaries*, because they bound it or limit it; just as the garden-walls all round it bound or shut in a house. Sometimes a range of mountains, sometimes a stream of water, divides one country from another; but often there is no mark of this kind to show the boundary line.

The people of the same country usually speak the same language. We can understand the talk of the people in any part of England. Though north country folk and west country folk have many queer words, still they all speak the *English language*.

English is spoken also in the country to the north of England, called Scotland, and in the country to the west of England, called Ireland, and, indeed, in many parts of the world, in countries which belong to England. If we crossed the English Channel we should be in another country which does not belong to England; and at first it would sound odd to hear the little children speaking in a tongue quite strange to us.

The people of the same country are generally governed by the same laws, and have the same king or queen or council over them.

A country which has a king or queen is called a *kingdom*. Our Queen has other countries besides England in her kingdom; a kingdom may include more than one country. If a kingdom be very large it is sometimes called an *empire*. Our Queen has been lately called Empress of India, because India consists of a great many kingdoms.

A country, which has no king, but is governed by a council chosen by the people from among themselves, is a *republic*.

The people of a country are usually noted for some particular qualities. One country will be famous for cleanliness; another, for industry; another for cleverness and wit.

English people are generally thought to be brave and truthful.

Also, the people of each country have ways of their own; ways of dressing, eating, cooking their food, and so on. The habits of a country depend a good deal upon its distance from the equator. People do not wear the same clothes, or eat the same sort of food in a hot country as in a cold one.

The countries of Europe are more civilised than those of any other part of the world, excepting America. That is, the people know better what is right and wrong; they behave more properly; send their children to school, and so are better educated; and know how to do their work in a better way. They also care more about books and reading, and are kinder in their ways to one another; they are so at least in Christian countries.

Most countries are divided into several smaller parts; in England these parts are called *counties*.

There are always *towns* in a country, many or few. If the country be rich and civilised like our own England, it has a great many

large towns. If it be a wild, waste country,
the map will only show a few towns scattered
here and there.

Most towns have several streets with houses
and shops. They have churches and schools,
factories and markets. Large towns have
very many streets and many people living in
them. The largest and most handsome town
in a country is generally the *capital* or chief
town. It has wide streets, often crowded
with gay carriages, handsome buildings, fine
shops, and rich people living in or near it.
There is generally a palace for the king in
or near the capital city of a country.

Towns upon the sea-coast, where the water
runs into the land, are often very busy. They
are *sea-ports*, with many ships coming and
going or resting in harbour. *Harbour* is the
name given to a small inlet where ships may
lie in shelter from the storms of the open sea.

By the *army* of a country, we mean the
soldiers who are kept ready to fight if that
country should go to war with another.

The *navy* means ships full of fighting men,
used when battles are fought upon the sea.

Questions on Lesson **XXXVIII**.

1. What is generally meant by a country?—A portion of land where the people speak the same language and are governed by the same laws.

2. What are the boundaries of a country?—The lands or waters which border it all round.

3. What is a kingdom?—The country or countries ruled by one king.

4. What is a republic?—A country ruled by a council chosen by the people.

5. What is a capital city?—Generally the largest and handsomest town in a country.

6. What is a sea-port?—A town on the coast to which ships come and go.

7. What is a harbour?—An inlet of the sea which affords shelter to ships.

8. What is an army?—The soldiers of a country.

9. What is a navy?—The war ships of a country.

LESSON XXXIX.

THE WATERS OF THE EARTH.

PART I.

LAND folk know little about the sea compared with the men who go down to the sea in ships and occupy their business upon the great deep. Still, people who have been to the sea-side know something about it. They have felt the delightful breeze that comes off the water;—a strong wind, sometimes, which blows off hats, sends hair flying about, and drives everybody along before it. What waves

SEA-SIDE VIEW.

there are in such a wind! high enough sometimes to wash over the pier. Great grey waves they are, which rise higher and higher until each long swell breaks into foam at the top; and then, how the white horses come galloping in to shore! And how the sea changes colour! At one time it is blue; then, a beautiful clear

I

green, flecked all over with white foam; and then, a dull, sad-looking grey.

Never still for a moment, it is always moving, always changing, always sending forth a sound. The least breath of wind spreads a ripple over the waters; and, wind or no wind, every day, wave after wave, the sea comes close in to the land. Then, as if shy of the land folk, it retires a long way off, leaving the sands wet and shining where it has been. No sooner is it out than it returns, but returns only to retire again.

This change goes on continually, twice every day, and is known as the coming in and going out, or the flow and ebb, of the *tide*.

When the tide is going out is the best time to hunt for sea-side treasures; lovely shells and curious sea-weed, strange-looking star-fish, and droll little crabs. But the fishing smacks bring in better treasures than these;— great boat-loads of herrings or mackerel, or other wholesome fish.

Then, who does not know the pleasure of bathing, of tumbling about in the cool water on a hot day? But how salt and bittert he water is which gets into our mouths.

So even landsmen know a good deal about the sea. They know how it looks, stretching away and away until it seems to touch the sky in a half circle. They have seen the ships come and go upon it, now sinking below, now rising above the half circle of the horizon. They know that the waters are salt and bitter. That the sea breezes bring health to the land. That the waters are never at rest, but are rippled, or raised into storm waves by the wind, and are always moving to and fro with the tide. That many fishes live in the waters, some with a shell for a house, and some only covered with shining scales. That curious plants, which we call sea-weeds, grow in the sea; and that its colour changes many times a day.

LESSON XL.

THE WATERS OF THE EARTH.

PART II.

But think what it would be to cross the great ocean in one of the ships we see sinking below the horizon. *Ocean* is the name given

to the mighty waters which cover so much
of the earth's surface. Think of sailing on,
day after day, week after week, and never
seeing land, nothing anywhere, but the wide
waste of waters. There is not half a circle,
but the whole circle of the horizon about you
everywhere, for nothing breaks the view.

A ROUGH SEA.

Wherever you look, water and sky seem to
meet in the far distance.

In the morning you see the sun rising,
it would seem, out of the sea in the east; and
you can easily watch him all day until he
seems to sink into the sea again in the west.

Now and then another ship crosses your
way and is "spoken," as sailors say.

Sad it is for all on board when a terrible storm arises! When the great billows mount higher than the ship's masts, and wash her decks, and cause the ship to reel to and fro, and fill her with water, until at last she sinks to the bottom.

If a ship goes to the bottom in mid-ocean, there is no hope of getting her up again. She will go down, down, to a greater depth in the water than you can imagine before the bottom is reached.

Think of the longest walk you are yet able to take, say five or six miles. Think of that long walk turned on end, so that you could go straight down the whole way as a fly might walk down a wall. Such a distance off, straight down, does the bottom or bed of the ocean lie.

This ocean bed is not flat, like the floor of a room; it rises into high places, and sinks down into low places as the surface of the land does.

Indeed many of these high places in the bed of the ocean rise to a height of more than five or six miles, and may be seen above the water, when they form islands. Sometimes these islands appear only as bare rocks, but sometimes trees and plants grow, and people live upon them.

The land stretching down into the great ocean divides it into separate parts, and each of these divisions is a little different from the others, and has a name of its own. In this way there are five oceans, though their waters unite and make the one great ocean, as you will see on a map or globe.

Questions on Lesson XL.

1. What is an ocean?—Ocean is the name of the great waters of the earth.

2. How many oceans are there?—Five.

3. How so?—The great ocean has five parts with different names.

4. Name the five oceans.—The Pacific, Atlantic, Indian, Arctic, and Antarctic.

LESSON XLI.

THE OCEANS AND THEIR PARTS.

THE ocean waters which surround each of the poles are frozen to a great depth. Even in the long summer day of those regions, when the sun does not set for months together, it fails to thaw the deep ice upon these frozen oceans.

Though the ice is never really thawed, yet the sun is strong enough to cause it to crack here and there with a sound like thunder. The great masses of ice,—icebergs, or ice mountains,—which are broken off in this way, float about where they can find room. Some of them make their way far north or south towards the equator; and ships' crews are sometimes startled to see a huge blue iceberg floating down upon them in quite warm regions. In the Polar regions multitudes of these ice mountains break loose in the summer; and these strike against one another every now and then with a tremendous crash.

You would think no vessel would venture into these terrible seas; yet, every few years ships full of brave men set forth to explore the Arctic Ocean.

The Arctic is the ocean about the North Pole. The ocean round the South Pole, the Antarctic, is even more dreary than the Arctic, because it is farther from inhabited lands.

The word Antarctic means "opposite to" the Arctic.

The great whale loves to bring up her young in these lonely seas.

The greatest of the oceans is the Pacific. It fills more space than all the countries of the earth taken together.

AN ISLAND.

It reaches south to the Antarctic, and the waters of these two oceans are not separated in any way. It is nearly divided from the Arctic by the northern lands of Asia and America, but there is a narrow passage of water which joins the two oceans. Such a narrow passage of water joining two larger portions is called a *strait*.

The high parts of the ocean bed rise above water in many places in the Pacific. These are called islands. An *island* is just a piece of land with water all round it. On the map you will find many islands scattered over the Pacific Ocean. They are mostly small and lie in *groups*; that is, several clustered together.

This ocean makes its way into the land in only one place on the American coast, by a long narrow opening called a *gulf*.

It has made five large openings on the eastern side of Asia, and each of these openings is separated from the rest of the ocean waters by a chain of islands.

Parts of the ocean lying in great curves of the land in this way are called *seas*, and the Pacific has five seas on the east of Asia.

The Atlantic Ocean is much smaller than the Pacific, but is more important to us. English ships are continually coming and going upon it, and can get into other oceans only after crossing the Atlantic.

Though it has not many ocean islands, the Atlantic has numerous large islands lying off the continents. It has also many inland seas; that is, seas which are nearly surrounded by land, not just locked in by a chain of islands. Some of these seas are connected with the ocean only by narrow *straits*; others, by wide passages of water called *channels*.

A STRAIT.

Sometimes the ocean enters the land by a wide opening not shut in in any way; such an opening is called a *bay*.

The Indian Ocean, which lies to the south of Asia, is the hottest of the oceans.

Questions on Lesson XLI.

1. What is a sea?—A part of the ocean lying in great curves of the land, or nearly surrounded by land.

2. What is a gulf?—An opening into the land, generally long and narrow.

3. What is a strait?—A narrow passage of water, joining two larger portions together.

4. What is a channel?—A passage of water generally longer and wider than a strait.

5. What is a bay?—An opening into the land, generally wide.

6. What is an island?—Land surrounded by water.

7. What is a group of islands?—Several islands lying close together.

8. What is the mainland?—The principal land, the continent.

9. What is a peninsula?—Land which the sea *almost* surrounds.

10. What is an isthmus?—The narrow neck of land which sometimes joins a peninsula to the mainland.

11. What is a cape?—A small piece of land jutting out into the sea. .

12 By what other names is such a point of land known?—Ness or Naze (which means nose), and point: a high cliff jutting into the sea is called a head or promontory.

Map Questions.

1. Between what continents does the Pacific lie?

2. The Atlantic?

3. The Indian Ocean?

4. What continents have shores washed by the Arctic Ocean?

5. Name the five seas east of Asia.

6. What strait connects the Pacific and Arctic Oceans?.

7. Name the gulf on the west of America.

8. Name a large bay on the west of Europe.

9. Name three large islands in the Mediterranean sea.

10. What channel lies between England and France?

11. What is the narrowest part of this channel called?

12. Name four large peninsulas which form part of the continent of Europe?

13. What isthmus connects Africa with Asia?

14. Name the most northerly cape in Europe.

15. The most southerly.

LONDON: PRINTED BY EDWARD STANFORD, 55, CHARING CROSS, S.W.

CPSIA information can be obtained
at www.ICGtesting.com
Printed in the USA
BVHW070117190919
558797BV00003B/131/P